(12⁵⁰) LINCOLN CHRISTIAN COLLEGE
5/82

D1072126

AMERICAN PSALMODY

Da Capo Press Music Reprint Series

GENERAL EDITOR

FREDERICK FREEDMAN

VASSAR COLLEGE

AMERICAN PSALMODY

or

Titles of Books Containing Tunes
Printed in America
From 1721 to 1820

Compiled by Frank J. Metcalf

New Introduction by Harry Eskew
New Orleans Baptist Theological Seminary

𝄞 DA CAPO PRESS · NEW YORK · 1968

A Da Capo Press Reprint Edition

This Da Capo Press edition of *American Psalmody* is an unabridged
republication of the first edition published in New York in 1917 in
an edition of eighty-one copies.

Library of Congress Catalog Card Number 68-13274

Copyright © 1968 by Da Capo Press
A Division of Plenum Publishing Corporation
227 West 17th Street
New York, N.Y. 10011

All rights reserved

Printed in the United States of America

INTRODUCTION

Frank Johnson Metcalf was born in Ashland, Massachusetts, on April 4, 1865. He acquired a Bachelor of Arts degree from Boston University in 1886, and taught school in Vermont, Texas, Utah, and Massachusetts before moving to Washington, D. C., in 1893. There he was employed in the Adjutant General's Office of the War Department as a research and correspondence clerk in charge of records for the Revolutionary War, the War of 1812, and the Mexican War. He held this position for a period of forty-two years, in the interim surviving the catastrophic collapse of the old Ford Theater Building on June 9, 1893, and raising a family of three children. Metcalf remained in Washington after his retirement in 1935, and died there on February 25, 1945.

During his years in the Capital, Metcalf led a multi-faceted life, becoming deeply involved in hymnology, religious affairs, bibliography, book collecting, and genealogy. His religious activity centered around the Brightwood Park Methodist Church, which he helped found in 1902, and which he served for more than forty years, while his genealogical pursuits included recording all birth, marriage, and death notices in the records of his home town, Ashland, Massachusetts, from 1846 through 1937.

As a book collector, Metcalf amassed an immense library of approximately six thousand religious works, among them a rare sixteenth-century Geneva Bible and a copy of that scarce eighteenth-century American tunebook, James Lyons' *Urania* (1761); and during several decades of research, he compiled a handwritten hymnal-tunebook bibliography listing some ten thousand items, and built up a private collection of more than two thousand

65098

American tunebooks and hymnals. Both his manuscript bibliography and his collection of musical books, including *Urania,* are now in the library of the American Antiquarian Society, making that institution perhaps the richest American repository of source material for the study of early American sacred music.

What we would describe today as "professional activity" was for Metcalf purely a labor of love; yet he earned the unequivocal respect of his professional colleagues, serving as vice-president of the Hymn Society of America and frequently as an invited member of the National Genealogical Society, American Antiquarian Society, American Historical Association, Bibliographical Society of America, and American Musicological Society.

In his early work Metcalf devoted himself to research and writing on the history of hymn texts. When, around 1915, he discovered the shortage of available historical information on hymn tunes, he turned his energies to research in early American sacred music. The results of his labors here were published in three volumes which are standard today: *American Psalmody* (New York, 1917), *American Writers and Compilers of Sacred Music* (New York, 1925), and *Stories of Hymn Tunes* (New York, 1928). In addition, Metcalf wrote numerous articles for a variety of journals.

Stories of Hymn Tunes includes historical data on fifty-four tunes by American composers; Metcalf's first two works are more extensive and represent his major contribution to American musical scholarship.

American Writers and Compilers of Sacred Music remains an essential source of basic biographical and bibliographical information on American sacred music and its composers during the eighteenth and nineteenth centuries, although scholars have since produced several specialized studies which supersede it in part. Here, as elsewhere, Metcalf was not concerned with questions of musical style; his approach was strictly bio-bibliographical, and many aspects of his studies have stood the test of time exceedingly well.

American Psalmody is a bibliography listing the short titles and library locations of more than two hundred books containing sacred music which were published in America in the eighteenth and early nineteenth centuries. (Although Metcalf's basic cut-off date is 1820, a few titles, as well as many later editions of pre-1820 works, extend beyond this date.) With few exceptions, the books listed are essential documents of the American singing-school tradition—a movement which received its main impetus in New England during the second and third decades of the eighteenth century, when regular singing became part of the reform movement in that region. These singing-school manuals, which typically open with a section on "musical rudiments" and contain upwards of several hundred harmonized tunes and anthems, are more commonly known as tunebooks. Thus, although psalmody was a prime force in American music for over a century, the use of this term in Metcalf's title may be slightly misleading, for by the late eighteenth century tunebooks were no longer restricted to settings of metrical psalms.

American Psalmody remains at this time the only published bibliography of American tunebooks extending through 1820. A much more comprehensive listing, based on Metcalf's manuscript bibliography and covering tunebooks, psalters, and hymnals through 1875, has been in progress for several years under the auspices of the American Antiquarian Society, but the Society's director, Marcus A. McCorison, reports that this bibliography, though nearly complete, remains unfinished because of the death of its compiler, Valmore X. Goucher. Lack of staff time has limited further work on it, and the American Antiquarian Society has been unable to schedule it for publication.

For the present, then, *American Psalmody* remains a basic tool for students of early American music, but three more recent bibliographies are essential as supplements. The first is Charles Evans' monumental *American Bibliography*.[1] This is particularly important for the years 1793–1800, since the volumes for these years appeared after the publication of *American Psalmody*.

Second, and more complete than the Evans work, is the specialized bibliography which forms a large part of Allen P. Britton's doctoral dissertation, *Theoretical Introductions in American Tunebooks to 1800* (University of Michigan, 1949).[2] Even though it is now almost twenty years old, Britton's study is still the most essential single source for accurate and reasonably complete bibliographical information on American tunebooks through 1800.

Finally, for the period from 1801 to 1819, *American Bibliography: A Preliminary Checklist*, by Ralph R. Shaw and Richard H. Shoemaker,[3] should be consulted. Although this work was compiled primarily from secondary sources, its coverage of tunebooks published in the first two decades of the nineteenth century is more complete than Metcalf's. Nevertheless, it complements rather than replaces the Metcalf, for each work contains titles and library locations not cited in the other.

Half a century has passed since the initial publication of *American Psalmody;* consequently, changes in library locations and major advances in American musical scholarship should be taken into account by those who use this book. For example, the Methodist Historical Society library in Boston has been incorporated

---

[1] *American Bibliography: A Chronological Dictionary of All Books, Pamphlets and Periodical Publications Printed in the United States of America From the Genesis of Printing in 1639 to and Including the Year 1820,* 14 volumes (1903–1959). This great work actually concludes with the material for the year 1800 contained in Volume 13 (prepared by C. K. Shipton). Publications for the years 1793–1800, inclusive, are listed in Volumes 9 through 13.

[2] A xerox copy or microfilm of this work can be obtained from University Microfilms, Inc., Ann Arbor, Michigan.

[3] *American Bibliography, A Preliminary Checklist for 1801–* (New York, The Scarcrow Press, 1958–). A continuation of Evans, this work is still in progress.

into the Boston University School of Theology library; the congregational Library is currently located at 14 Beacon Street, Boston; the John Carter Brown Library of Providence, Rhode Island, has become part of the Brown University Libraries; and that portion of the Warrington Collection cited by Metcalf is now in the library of the Pittsburgh Theological Seminary.[4]

American Psalmody also seems to have perpetrated a number of bibliographical "ghosts." Britton, for instance, questions the existence of the 1769 edition of Bayley's *New Universal Harmony* (page 13, below), of Jocelyn's *Federal Harmony* (page 32), and of the 1778 edition of Mann's *Northampton Collection* (page 38). As a general rule, the reader is advised to exercise greatest caution with regard to items which fail to indicate library locations; thus, it would be pointless to look for the above three items, or even to consider Howe's *Divine Hymns* (page 30), which, according to Britton, is no tunebook at all, but rather a collection of hymns without music.

Naturally, many more American tunebooks issued prior to 1820 have been located since *American Psalmody* first appeared. This is particularly true in the case of the earliest Southern shape-note tunebooks, which were first explored in detail by George Pullen Jackson in *White Spirituals in the Southern Uplands* (1933).[5] At least five shape-note tunebooks (including Davisson's *Kentucky Harmony* of 1816) in seven editions appeared in the Shenandoah Valley of Virginia, alone, between 1816 and 1820, and none are recorded in *American Psalmody*. Most of the

---

[4] A strong indication of the increasing interest in early American sacred music is the development of significant collections of early American tunebooks by a number of other institutions. Four of these are worthy of special mention: The Pace Memorial Library of Hartford Theological Seminary, Hartford, Connecticut, which includes a large part of the Warrington Collection; the Library of the Union Theological Seminary, New York, New York; the Library of the Moravian Music Foundation, Winston-Salem, North Carolina, which houses the Irving Lowens Collection; and the Libraries of the University of California at Los Angeles, which contain the collections of George Pullen Jackson and Royal Stanton.

[5] Chapel Hill, University of North Carolina Press.

missing titles, however, may be found in the Evans, Britton, or Shaw-Shoemaker bibliographies. Information on post-1820 tunebooks can be obtained from the library of Congress, through its National Union Catalog, and from the American Antiquarian Society's Goucher Catalog.

While its shortcomings are quite apparent, Metcalf's *American Psalmody* is still the only published bibliography of American tunebooks covering the entire period through 1820; as such, it remains a convenient and useful reference work for serious students of American musical history.

New Orleans   HARRY ESKEW
May, 1967

AMERICAN PSALMODY

THE

New-England PSALM-SINGER :

O R,

American CHORISTER.

C O N T A I N I N G

A Number of PSALM-TUNES, ANTHEMS AND CANONS.

In Four and Five Parts.

[*Never before Publifhed.*]

Compofed by WILLIAM BILLINGS,

A Native of BOSTON, in *New-England.*

MATTHEW xxi. 16. — *Out of the Mouth of Babes and Sucklings thou haft perfected Praife.*
JAMES v. 13. —— *Is any Merry ? Let him fing Pfalms.*

O praife the Lord with one Confent, and in this grand Defign,
Let Britain and the Colonies, unanimoufly join.

BOSTON : *New-England.* Printed by EDES and GILL.

And to be Sold by them at their Printing-Office in Queen-Street ; by Deacon *Elliot*, under Liberty-Tree ;
by *Jofiah Flagg*, in Fifh-Street ; by *Gillam Bafs*, the Corner of Ann-Street, and by the Author.

[Price Eight Shillings, L. M.]

New England Psalm Singer, 1770, by William Billings
From copy in the Library of Congress

AMERICAN PSALMODY

OR

TITLES OF BOOKS, CONTAINING TUNES

PRINTED IN AMERICA

FROM 1721 TO 1820

Compiled by

FRANK J. METCALF, A. B.

Member of the American Historical Association

ILLUSTRATED

Seventy-three Copies Published by

CHARLES F. HEARTMAN, New York City

For Subscribers only

1917

Bibliographical work is fascinating for him who happens to be afflicted with the disease; it is stupid work in the eyes of him who is not, but it becomes useful work in the eyes of even the scoffers if circumstances compel them to depend upon a piece of bibliographical work well done.

From Sonneck's "History of Music in America," a paper read before the Music Teachers National Association, 1916.

PREFACE

This list of American books of Sacred Music is intended to cover the period from the first one printed in English by Rev. John Tufts, in or about 1721, to and including the year 1820. Its basis is the list of "Short Titles" printed privately in 1898 by James Warrington, (since deceased) of Philadelphia, Pa. To those given by him many have been added as they have been discovered in the many libraries which have been examined. The abbreviations used in locating copies are as follows:

AAS	American Antiquarian Society	Worcester, Mass.
BPL	Boston Public Library	Boston, Mass.
BU	Brown University	Providence, R. I.
Catalogue	Titles taken from sales catalogues	
Congl	Congregational Library	Boston, Mass.
Conn.	See Note	
CR	Titles from Copyright Records	Washington, D. C.
EI	Essex Institute	Salem, Mass.
Evans	American Bibliography by Charles Evans	Chicago, Ill.
Harv	Harvard Musical Association	Boston, Mass.
HU	Harvard University	Cambridge, Mass.
JCB	John Carter Brown Library	Providence, R. I.
LM	Lowell Mason Collection in Yale University	New Haven, Conn.
LOC	Library of Congress	Washington, D. C.
Maine	See Note	
MdHS	Maryland Historical Society	Baltimore, Md.
Meth	Methodist Historical Society	Boston, Mass.
MHS	Massachusetts Historical Society	Boston, Mass.
NECons	New England Conservatory of Music	Boston, Mass.
NL	Newberry Library	Chicago, Ill.
NYPL	New York Public Library	New York, N. Y.
NY	See Note	
Oberlin	Oberlin College	Oberlin, O.
Penn	See Note	
PHS	Pennsylvania Historical Society	Philadelphia, Pa.
Priv	Titles from books in private collections	
RIHS	Rhode Island Historical Society	Providence, R. I.
Utica	Public Library	Utica, N. Y.
Va	See Note	
Yale	Yale Library	New Haven, Conn.
WR	Western Reserve Historical Society	Cleveland, Ohio
W	Warrington Collection in Western Theological Seminary	Pittsburgh, Pa.

NOTE: When the name of a state appears between the date of copyright and the letters CR, e. g. c1814 Conn CR, it is to be read: copyright entered in District of Conn. as shown by Copyright Record.

I have undertaken to locate all the copies examined, but the shortcomings in this respect are many. This is explained by the fact that when the writer began to make notes, it was with no thought that they would ever see the light of print, and much data that now would seem valuable was omitted as not necessary to the object then in view. Many of the original books are now inaccessible, scattered in many cities and states, and, therefore, many such items must be left out.

Unstinted courtesy has been extended to every request for consultation of the collections in the various libraries visited. I must not, however, omit special reference to Mr. O. G. Sonneck and his several assistants in the Music Division of the Library of Congress, where the greater part of my work has been done, for the assistance and suggestions so freely offered. A list of music copyrights, made for the use of that Division, was placed at my disposal, and I there found the only evidence of the existence of a number of titles which I have indicated by the name of the state in which recorded, and the letters "CR" (Copyright Record). To the keen insight and large experience of Mr. Sonneck are also due the solution of several bibliographical puzzles.

No effort has been made to investigate the German books prepared for the communities in and around Ephrata, Pennsylvania, nor the productions of the Saur Press. This is a subject worthy of extended study, and must be left to other hands.

As to the shapes of the books I have designated only two,—oblong which are wider than they are tall, and 8vo, the shape of the common hymnal,—taller than wide.

While the brevity of the titles forbids full explanations of the differences of editions, it is hoped that the information given will be sufficient to identify the individual books that make up the collection of sacred music of the eighteenth century.

FRANK J. METCALF.

Washington, D. C., October 15, 1917.

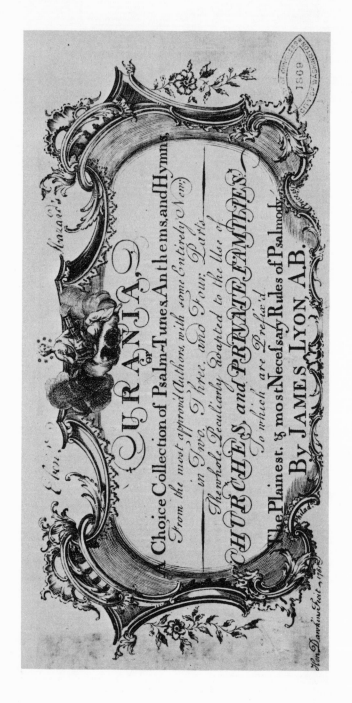

Urania, 1761, by James Lyon
From copy in the Library of Congress

COLLECTIONS OF AMERICAN PSALMODY

1721-1820

ABBOTT, C. C.

The Young Converts Pocket Companion with tunes

| | Boston | 1822 | Meth |

ADDINGTON, STEPHEN

Sacred Music, No. 1 containing Psalm and Gymn Tunes now
used at the Independent Tabernacle at Philadelphia,

| | c1807 | Penn | CR |

Valuable Selection of Psalm and Hymn Tunes

| | Philadelphia | 1808 | Phil | Lib Co |

(Perhaps identical with the above)

ADGATE, ANDREW

Philadelphia Harmony,

56p. obl.	Philadelphia	1788	LOC
Second ed.	Philadelphia		
Third ed. 20-56p.obl.	Philadelphia	1790	AAS LOC

(The first copyright under Federal law.)

Fourth ed.	Philadelphia	1791	
Fifth ed.	Philadelphia		
Sixth ed.	Philadelphia	1799	
Seventh ed.	Philadelphia	1801	LM
Eighth ed.	Philadelphia	1803	
Part 1 and 2 110p. obl.	Philadelphia	n. d.	WR
Rudiments of Music, obl.	Philadelphia	1788	Evans
Second ed.	Philadelphia		

Third ed., 20, 56p.

obl.	Philadelphia	1790	LOC
Fourth ed. 102p. obl.	Philadelphia	1796	W
Fifth ed.	Philadelphia		
Sixth ed. 110p. obl.	Philadelphia	1799	W
Seventh ed.	Philadelphia		
Eighth ed.	Philadelphia	1803	

A Selection of Sacred Harmony

84p. of music	Philadelphia	1788	LOC
Second ed.	Philadelphia	1789	
Third ed.	Philadelphia	1790	
Fourth ed.	Philadelphia	1794	
Fifth ed.	Philadelphia	1797	

Select Psalms and Hymns

	Philadelphia	1787	Evans
Uranian Instructions, 12p.	Philadelphia	1787	LOC
bound in with a Selec-			
tion of Sacred Harmony, 1788			

ADGATE AND HUSBAND

The Philadelphia Harmony		c1808	Penn	CR
110p. obl.	Philadelphia	n. d.	W	

AITKEN, JOHN

Litanies and Vesper Hymns and Anthems

	Philadelphia	1787	
Second ed. 181p.	Philadelphia	1791	JCB

ALBEE, AMOS, (1772-18—).

Norfolk Collection

48p. obl.	Dedham	1805	LOC

See also Oliver Shaw.

ALLEN, FRANCIS D.

New York Selection of Sacred Music

	New York	1818

10

Second ed. 6, 221, 2p.

obl.	New York	1822	Priv
Third ed.	New York	1823	LM

Fourth stereotyped ed.

8, 221p. obl.	New York	1826	Priv
Fifth ed.	New York		
Sixth ed.	New York		
Seventh ed.	New York	1828	MHS

Eighth stereotyped ed., enlarged and improved

obl.	New York	1833	LOC

Selection of Sacred music for the use of the Reformed
  Dutch Church in the City of New York

	c1818	NY CR

ANDERSON, REV. JOHN

  Vindicate Cantus Dominia

	Philadelphia	1793
Same		1800

ARMBRUSTER, ANTHONY

Tunes in Three Parts	Philadelphia	1763	
Second ed	Philadelphia	1764	HSP quoted by Evans

ARMSTRONG, JOHN

  Pittsburgh Selection of Psalm Tunes

111p. obl.	Pittsburgh	1816	LOC

ASPLUND, JOHN (17..-1807)

New Collection	Baltimore	1793

ATWELL, THOMAS H.

  New York Collection of Sacred Harmony, or
  New York and Vermont Collection   1794

Second ed. 112p. obl.	Albany	1804	AAS LOC
Same	Albany	1805	
Third ed.	Albany		

BABCOCK, SAMUEL
Middlesex Harmony	Watertown	1795	MHS
56p. obl.	Boston	1795	AAS LOC
Second ed.	Boston	1803	AAS BPL
			LOC LM

BAIRD, REV. T. D.
| Science of Praise | Zanesville, O. | 1816 | |

BALTIMORE COLLECTION OF SACRED MUSIC
| | Baltimore | 1792 | Evans |

BAYLEY, DANIEL (1725[?]-1799)

American Harmony—See Royal Melody Complete

American Harmony or Universal Psalmodist (A. Williams)

| 192p. obl. | Newburyport | 1769 | Catalogue |
| 84p. obl. | Newburyport | 1771 | Priv |

Same forming Part I of the Seventh ed. of The
Royal Melody Complete   1771
also Part II of the succeeding editions

Anthems and Hymn Tunes

	Newburyport	1784	Evans
Essex Harmony, 2,22p.	Newburyport	1770	BPL LOC
a copy bound with a Bible			NYPL
Same	Boston	1770	BPL LOC
Same, 2, 18p.	Boston	1771	AAS MHS
bound with a Tate and Brady			W
Same bound with a Tate and Brady of 1765			EI
Same bound with version of Psalms of 1772			AAS EI
Same with Watts' Psalms		1780	JCB
Same, 48p. obl.	Newburyport	1785	AAS EI
			NYPL W

New and Complete Introduction

| 20p. of music | Newburyport | 1764 | EI MHS |
| 28p. obl. | Boston | 1766 | BPL LM |

```
        36p.  obl.      Boston            1768  EI  LOC
New Harmony of Zion or Complete Melody
        100p.           Newburyport    1788  Evans
        112p.  obl.     Newburyport    1788  LOC
New Universal Harmony
                        Newburyport    1769
    Same 105p.          Newburyport    1773  BPL  MHS
Psalm Singers Assistant
        8,16p.          Newburyport    1765  BPL
    Imperfect copy bound with a Tate and Brady
                        Boston            1767  JCB
        24p.            Newburyport    1785  BPL
Royal Melody Complete, or New Harmony of Zion
    (William Tans'ur)
        (First American edition, called the third edition)
    Third ed. with additions
        96p.  obl.      Boston            1767  LOC
                                                NECons
    Fourth ed. 96p. obl.  Boston          1768
    Fifth ed.                             (1769)? LOC
    Sixth ed. 96p.  obl.  Boston          1771  JCB  LOC
        This and succeeding editions contained Aaron Williams'
            Universal Psalmodist which was designated Vol. II
            in the seventh and following editions.
    Seventh ed.         Newburyport    1771  LOC
    Eighth ed.          Newburyport    1773  LOC
                                                NYPL  W
    Ninth ed.           Newburyport    1774
BELCHER, SUPPLY (1751-1836)
    Harmony of Maine
        104p.  obl.     Boston            1794  AAS  BPL
                                          LM  MHS  NYPL  W
```

13

BELKNAP, DANIEL (1771-1815)
    Evangelical Harmony
76p.	Boston	1800	AAS BPL
	JCB	LM LOC MHS	NECons

    Harmonist's Companion

31p.	Boston	1797	AAS
Middlesex Collection	Boston	1802	AAS MHS
Second ed.		1808	LM
Middlesex Songster		c1809	Mass CR
Village Compilation	Boston	1806	AAS LM
			MHS
Second ed. 151p. obl.	Boston	1806	LOC

BENHAM, ASAHEL

Federal Harmony, 58p.	New Haven	1790	
130p. obl.	Boston	1790	BPL JCB
			LOC RIHS
Second ed.	New Haven	1792	Evans
Third ed.			
Fourth ed.			
Fifth ed.	Middletown	1794	
Sixth ed. 64p. obl.	Middletown	1795	LOC ‾
Hunting Song		c1814	Conn. CR
Social Harmony	Wallingford	1798	MHS
Same		1799	

BENJAMIN, JONATHAN
    Harmonia Cœlestis

80p. obl.	Northampton	1799	AAS BPL
			LOC

BILLINGS, WILLIAM (1742-1800)
    Continental Harmony

200p. obl.	Boston	1794	AAS EI
	BPL LM	LOC MHS	Congl

Easter Anthem, 8p. obl. Boston		n. d.	MHS
Music in Miniature			
32p.	Boston	1779	BPL
			LM (imp)
New England Psalm Singer			
108p. obl.	Boston	1770	BPL LM
			LOC MHS
Psalm Singers Amusement			
103p. obl.	Boston	1781	BPL LOC
			MHS
Singing Master's Assistant			
32, 104p. obl.	Boston	1778	BPL EI
			LOC MHS
Second ed.			
32, 104p. obl.	Boston	1779	Evans NL
Third ed.	Boston	1781	EI LM
			MHS RIHS
Suffolk Harmony			
56p. obl.	Boston	1786	AAS LOC
			MHS

BLAKE, GEORGE E. (1775-1871)

Blake's Military Amusement			
Marches, quicksteps, etc.		c1813	Penn. CR
Blake's Musical Miscellany for the pianoforte			
		c1815	Penn. CR
Vocal Harmony, 68p.	Philadelphia	1810	LM LOC

BLANCHARD, AMOS

American Musical Primer			
88p. obl.	Exeter	1808	LM LOC
			NYPL
Newburyport Collection			
151p. obl.	Exeter	1807	BPL LM
			LOC NYPL

112p. obl.   Boston   (ca 1800) BPL LOC
Brattle Street Collection—See Nahum Mitchell
Bridgewater Collection

(The first and second editions were called The Columbian
and European Harmony, or Bridgewater Collection,
later editions Templi Carmina, or Bridgewater Collection)

159p. obl.	Boston	1802	AAS	BPL
				LOC
Second ed. 167p. obl.	Boston	1804	AAS	BPL
				LOC
Third ed.	Boston	1810	AAS	BPL
				MHS
Fourth ed. 321p. obl.	Boston	1816	BPL	LOC
				MHS
Fifth ed. 325p. obl.	Boston	1817	Congl	LOC
Sixth ed. improved and enlarged				
325, 3p. obl.	Boston	1818	BPL	
Seventh ed. 325p. obl.	Boston	1819	BPL	LOC
				NYPL
Eighth ed. 325p. obl.	Boston	1820	LM	LOC
				NYPL W
Ninth ed.	Boston	1821	BPL	LM
				RIHS
Tenth ed. 333p. obl.	Boston	1822	LOC	NYPL
Eleventh ed.				
Twelfth ed.	Boston	1823	LM	NYPL
				RIHS
Thirteenth ed.				
333p. obl.	Boston	1824	LOC	
Fourteenth ed.				
336p. obl.	Boston	1824	Congl	W

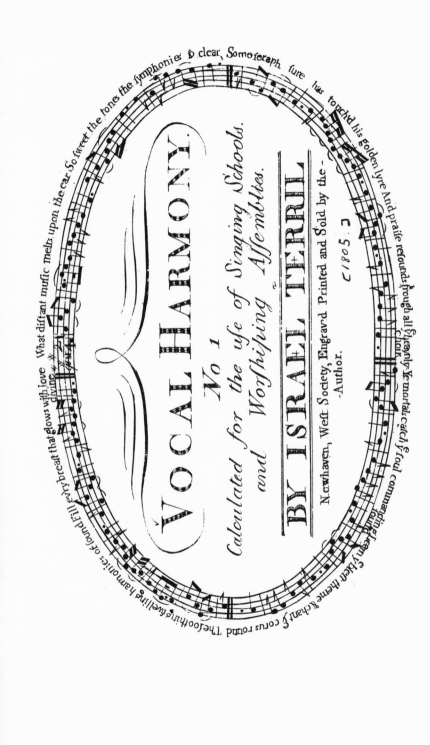

VOCAL HARMONY.

No 1

Calculated for the use of Singing Schools. and Worshiping Assemblies.

BY ISRAEL TERRIL

Newhaven, West Society, Engravd Printed and Sold by the -Author.

C 1805]

Vocal Harmony, No. I, by Israel Terril

From copy in the Library of Congress

The owner of this copy put in the date Dec. 25. 1805

Fifteenth ed.

     337p. obl.   Boston   1825 LOC NYPL

Sixteenth ed.

     337p. obl.   Boston   1826 LOC NYPL

Seventeenth ed.

Eighteenth ed.   Boston   1828

Nineteenth ed.   Boston   1829 LM

Twentieth ed.

     349(3) obl.   Boston   1830 Oberlin

Twenty-first ed.

     349p. obl.   Boston   1831 LOC

Twenty-second ed.   Boston   1832 Congl

Twenty-third ed.

     349p. obl.   Boston   1833 Congl LOC

Twenty-fourth ed.

     349p. obl.   Boston   1834 LOC

Twenty-fifth ed.

Twenty-sixth ed.

     349p. obl.   Boston   1836 LM LOC

     Twenty-seventh ed. Boston   1839 MHS

BROWN, ALLING

    The Gamut, 22p.   New Haven   1823 BPL

    Musical Cabinet, or New Haven Collection

                    New Haven   1824 AAS

BROWNSON, OLIVER

    New Collection of Sacred Harmony

        56p. obl.   Simsbury, Conn. 1797 Priv

    Select Harmony

        84p. obl.   New Haven   1783 LOC MHS

                    New Haven   1791

       (An imperfect copy in MHS may be the 1791 edition)

BULL, AMOS
   The Responsary
            100p. obl.   Worcester   1795 BPL Congl
                                        LOC MHS NYPL W
BULL, WILLIAM (1762-1842)
   Music adapted to Language   c1813 Mass. CR
BUSHNELL, J.
   Musical Synopsis   Northampton   1807
BUTTS, THOMAS
   Harmonica Sacra   London   1770
            reprinted at   Andover   1816 AAS
CAPEN, SAMUEL
   Norfolk Harmony, No. 1 Anthems and Set Pieces
            63, 1p. obl.   Boston   1805 Priv
CARR, BENJAMIN (1769-1831)
   Chorister, or a Collection of Chants and Melodies
            36p.   Philadelphia   1820 LM
   Collection of Chants,
            62p.   Philadelphia   1816 LM
   Lessons and Exercises in Vocal Music
            60p. obl.   Baltimore   c1811 W
   Masses, Vespers and Litanies
            128p.   n. p.   1805 HSP
CARROLL, JAMES P.
   Songs of Zion, Tunes principally original
                                        c1820 Va. CR
CHANTS FOR THE PROTESTANT EPISCOPAL CHURCH 1823
CHAPIN, NATHAN, with Joseph L. Dickerson
   The Musical Instructer (sic)
            100p. obl.   Philadelphia   1810 LOC

CHILD, EBENEZER
   The Sacred Musician
           118p.   Boston   1804 AAS BPL
CHOICE COLLECTION   Philadelphia   1743
CHORISTERS' GUIDE, Music selected from the songs of the Temple
      with reference to Belknap's Psalms and Hymns
                                               c1818 Mass. CR
CHURCH MUSIC SELECTED BY A COMMITTEE
                              Hartford   1817
                              New London
CLIFTON, ARTHUR
   Original Psalm Tunes
           44 leaves, obl. Baltimore   1819 LM   Priv
COLE, ISAAC P.
   Third Presbyterian Church Collection
           92p.   Philadelphia   1815 title in W
   Pocket Edition of Psalm and Hymn Tunes
                              New York   1834 LM
      Second ed.
      Third ed.
      Fourth ed.
      Fifth ed. sm. obl.
           276p.   Albany   1835 LM   W
      Sixth ed.
      Seventh ed.
      Eighth ed.   Albany   1837 LM
      Ninth ed.
      Tenth ed. 300+p. obl. Albany   1839 Priv
COLE, JOHN (1774-1855)
   Beauties of Psalmody
      Second ed. 103p. obl. Baltimore   1805 W

19

Third ed., 89 pieces, index and 12p. chants for the Protestant Episcopal Church

	Baltimore	1827	Harv

Collection of Anthems

56p.	Baltimore	n. d.	LM

Collection of Psalm Tunes

55p.	Boston	1803	LM
Devotional Harmony	Baltimore	1814	LM

Divine Harmonist

56p. obl.	n. p.	1808	AAS
Ecclesiastical Harmony	Baltimore	1810	
Episcopalian Harmony	Baltimore	1800	
Same, 87p. obl.	Baltimore	c1811	LOC

Laudate Dominum (chants)

28p.	Baltimore	1842	LM
Second ed.			
Third ed.	Baltimore	1847	LM
Minstrel (songs), 316p.	Baltimore	1812	LOC

Sacred Melodies 1-3

24p.	Baltimore	1828	LM	
Seraph, 200p. obl.	Baltimore	1821	LM	W
Same	Baltimore	1822	Priv	
Same, 200p. obl.	Baltimore	1827	Harv	
			LM	W

Songs of Zion, Psalm Tunes

224p.	Baltimore	1818	LM

Union Harmony, patent notes

440p. obl.	Baltimore	1829	LM	LOC

COLLECTION OF PSALM, HYMN AND CHANT TUNES 1823
COLLECTION OF PSALM TUNES FOR CHRIST'S CHURCH AND ST. PETER'S in Philadelphia

9, 23p.		1763	PHS

COLLECTION OF SACRED MUSIC FOR CHURCHES WHICH SING WITHOUT
    A CHOIR   c1817 N.Y. CR
COLUMBIAN AND EUROPEAN HARMONY. First and second editions
    of the Bridgewater Collection appeared under this title
COLUMBIAN HARP, 80p. obl.   Northampton   1812 AAS
CONNECTICUT HARMONY--see Elijah Griswold
COOPER, WILLIAM

    Beauties of Church Music

199p. obl.	Boston	1804	AAS LM
			LOC RIHS

    Original Sacred Music, containing three pieces of music

12p.	Boston	n. d. c1803	LOC LM
Thanksgiving Anthem	Boston	1792	AAS LOC

DAVID'S COMPANION, or the Methodist Standard 1810—See James
    Evans
    Same   1811
DAVID'S HARP, 112 leaves, obl. Baltimore   1812 LM MdHS
DEERFIELD COLLECTION—See Samuel Willard
DICKERSON, JAMES L.

    The Musical Instructor, with Nathan Chapin
DOOLITTLE, AMOS (1754-1832) See Simeon Jocelyn
DYER, SAMUEL (1785-1835)

    New York Selection of Sacred Music
        132p., 94p. of anthems

obl.	Baltimore	1817	AAS LM

    Second ed.

244 pieces, obl.	Baltimore	1819	AAS
			Harv W

Third ed.	Baltimore	1824	
Fourth ed. obl.	New York	1828	LOC Oberlin
Fifth ed.			
Sixth ed. obl.	Philadelphia	n. d.	

21

Philadelphia Selection of Sacred music
Fourth ed. improved and enlarged
        obl.   New York   1828 LOC NYPL
                                               Priv   W
    Fifth ed.
    Sixth ed.   Philadelphia   n. d. Priv
Selection of Anthems, 94p. issued with
        his Sacred Music   1817
    Second ed. 204p. and supplement
        24p. obl.   Baltimore   1822 LOC LM
    Third ed. obl.   Philadelphia   1834 LM LOC
                                                 Oberlin
        (This edition has biographical notes of many of the
            composers)
    Fourth ed.
    Fifth ed.
    New Sixth ed. revised and corrected by his son,
        Samuel Owen Dyer,
            222p. and supplement 24p. obl.
                c1835 but printed at New York 1851
    A reprint by Ditson Co.
                        Boston (ca1870) c1834 BPL
    Choruses, Solos, &c. 1830 bound with Anthems,
                                        1834 NYPL
ECKHARD, J.
    Choral Book   Boston   1816
ERBAN, PETER (1769-1861)
    Select Psalm and Hymn Tunes
                        New York   1806
ESSEX HARMONY, Part 2,
        99p. obl.   Salem   1802 LM

22

EVANGELICAL SONGSTER   1812
EVANS, J.
    David's Companion   New York   1807 NYPL
      Same XII, 82p. obl.   New York   1808 W
                      Baltimore   1810
                             c1810 CR New York

EYER, J. F.—See I. Gerhart (1818)
FEDERAL HARMONY, 112p.   Boston   1790 JCB
FIRST CHURCH COLLECTION   Boston   1806 BPL
    Second ed. 136p.   Boston   1815 BPL Harv
                                    MHS W

           94p. 8vo.   Boston   1815 LOC
FLAGG, JOSIAH
    Collection of Best Psalm Tunes
           65p. obl.   Boston   1764 LOC NYPL
    Sixteen Anthems, 70p.   Boston   (1766?) LOC
FLINT, TIMOTHY
    Columbian Harmonist, patent notes
          204p.   Cincinnati   1816 Harv
FOBES, AZARIAH
    Delaware Harmony   Philadelphia   1809 NL
FORBUSH, ABIJAH
    Psalmodist's Assistant
        68p.   Boston   1803 AAS
    Second ed. 108p.   Boston   1806 AAS
                                  MHS NYPL

FRAZEE, JOHN—See John W. Nevius
FRENCH, JACOB (1754- ?)
    Harmony of Harmony
         150p. obl.   Northampton   1802 AAS LOC
                                  MHS NYPL

New American Melody

100p.	Boston	1789	AAS

Psalmodist's Companion

obl.	Worcester	1793	AAS	LOC

FROST, RUFUS

Medford Harmony, 23p.	Boston	1805	BPL

FRISBIE, JOHN C.—See Stephen Jenks

GAMUT OR SCALE OF MUSIC

obl.	Hartford	1788	Evans
obl.	Hartford	1805	NYPL

(This copy belonged to Oliver Ditson)

24p. obl.	Hartford	1807	LOC	
	Hartford	1811	BPL	
32p. obl.	Hartford	1814	AAS	LOC
obl.	Utica	1815		
8vo.	Utica	1815		

Published at Hartford but printed at New London

		1816	LM
		1816	Congl
obl.	Utica	1818	
8vo.	Utica	1818	
	Albany	n. d.	AAS

GARDINER, WILLIAM

Sacred Melodies from Handel, Mozart and Beethoven,

Vol. I		c1818	Penn CR

GERHART, I.

Choral Harmonie		1818	
Same	Harrisburg	1822	

GILLET. WHEELER, & Co.

Maryland Selection

86p. obl.	Baltimore	1809	BU	LOC

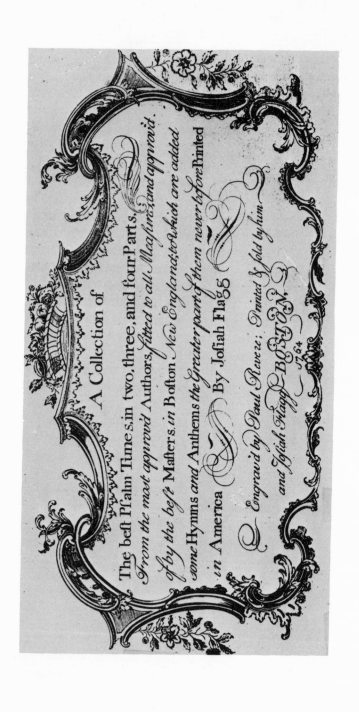

A Collection of

The best Pſalm Tunes, in two, three, and four Parts.
From the moſt approv'd Authors, fitted to all Meaſures, and approv'd.
of by the beſt Maſters, in Boſton New England; to which are added
ſome Hymns and Anthems the Greater part of them never before Printed
in America

By Joſiah Flagg

Engrav'd by Paul Revere; Printed & ſold by him
and Joſiah Flagg BOSTON.
1764

Collection of Psalm Tunes, 1764, by Josiah Flagg
From copy in the Library of Congress

45098

GOODALE, EZEKIEL (1780- ?)
Hallowell Collection
         200p. obl.   Hallowell, Me. 1817 AAS Congl
                             LOC LM MHS NYPL
    Second ed. 216p. obl. Hallowell, Me. 1819 MHS
GRAM, HANS
    Anthem for Easter   Charlestown 1794 MHS
    The Massachusetts Compiler, with Oliver Holden and
        Samuel Holyoke
         36,72p. obl.   Boston   1795 Congl LOC
                               LM MHS NYPL

    Sacred lines for Thanksgiving
                      Boston   1793 AAS MHS
GRISWOLD, ELIJAH—See Stephen Jenks
    The Hartford Collection Hartford   1807
GRISWOLD, ELIJAH AND SKINNER, THOMAS
    Connecticut Harmony
         54p. obl.   Hartford   1800 LOC
HALLOWELL COLLECTION—See E. Goodale
HARDY, DANIEL
    Thanksgiving Anthem   c1808 Mass. CR
HARMON, JOEL (1773-1833)
    Columbian Sacred Minstrel
         80p.   Northampton 1809
    Musical Primer   Harrisburg (ca1814)
HARMONICA SACRA
        243p. large sq. Andover   1816 AAS Congl
                                           NYPL
    (Reprint of the London edition of Thomas Butts)
HARTWELL, EDWARD
    Chorister's Companion
         166p.   Exeter   1815 BPL

HASTINGS, THOMAS (1784-1872)

Musica Sacra or Springfield and Utica Collections

	Utica	1816	
Rev. ed. 8vo.	Utica	1818	Oberlin
Second ed.			
Second rev. ed.			
280p. obl.	Utica	1818	AAS Congl LM LOC
Second ed. rev.			
280p. 8vo.	Utica	c1819	WR W
Second rev. ed.			
280p. obl.	Utica	1819	AAS BPL LOC Utica
Third rev. ed.			
280p. 8vo.	Utica	1822	AAS LOC WR
Fourth rev. ed.			
280p. 8vo.	Utica	1823(c1819)	AAS Utica Priv
Fifth rev. ed.			
264p. obl.	Utica	1825	LOC WR
Sixth ed. rev.			
264p. obl.	Utica	c1826 1827	Oberlin
Seventh rev. ed., obl.	Utica	1828	Priv
Eighth rev. ed.			
268p. obl.	Utica	1829	LM Priv
Ninth rev. ed., 286p.	Utica	1831	LOC LM
Ninth rev. ed. with additions and improvements			
	Utica	1832	Priv Oberlin W
Ninth rev. ed.		1833	Congl

Tenth rev. ed.

     300p. obl.   Utica   1834 (c1830) Utica   Priv

   Same with appendix of tunes

	Utica	1834	Priv
Tenth rev. ed.	Utica	1835	
Tenth rev. ed.	Utica	1836	Utica
Tenth rev. ed.	Utica	1838	
Musical Reader	Utica	1817	
Revised and enl.	Utica	1819	

Utica Collection. (This was the basis of the Musica Sacra.
   I have not seen a copy.)

HEWETT, JAMES

Harmonia Sacra, 120p. Boston   1812 AAS LM
                                        LOC NYPL W

HILL, URI K.

Handelian Repository New York   1814 LM
Sacred Minstrel, No. 1
    72p.   Boston   1806 AAS
                                        LM LOC

Solfeggio Americana New York   1820 NYPL
                                        LM LOC

Vermont Harmony,
    Vol. I, 80p.   Northampton 1801 W

HOLBROOK, JOSIAH, with David Pool

American and European Harmony
    208p. obl.   Providence   1813 BPL LM
                                  LOC MHS RIHS

HOLDEN, OLIVER (1765-1844)

American Harmony
    32p. obl.   Boston   1792 EI LOC
                                    LM MHS

Charlestown Collection
      80p.   Boston   1803 BPL

Massachusetts Compiler—See Hans Gram

Modern Collection of Sacred Music
      254p. obl.   Boston   1800 LOC

Occasional Pieces
      16p.   Boston   n. d. AAS

Plain Psalmody, 71p. Boston   1800 LOC
                                          MHS AAS

Sacred Dirges
      24p. obl.   Boston   1800 LOC MHS

Union Harmony, Vol. 1
      120p. obl.   Boston   1793 AAS LOC
                                          MHS NYPL

      Second ed.   Boston   1796 AAS
                                            EI MHS

      Third ed.   Boston   1801 Congl

Union Harmony, Vol. 2
      176p. obl.   Boston   1793 EI
                                          LOC MHS

Worcester Collection of Sacred Harmony—see Worcester
    Collection

HOLLIS STREET COLLECTION OF PSALM AND HYMN TUNES
      72p. obl.   Boston   1811 HU W

HOLT, BENJAMIN (1774-1861)
    New England Sacred Harmony
      56p. obl.   Boston   1803 AAS LOC
    Thanksgiving Hymn   1825 AAS

HOLYOKE, SAMUEL (1762-1820)
    Anthem for Fast Day   Salem   n. d. LM
    Christian Harmonist   Salem   1804 Congl LM
                                          LOC NYPL

Columbian Repository

471p. large obl.	Exeter	1802	AAS LOC	
			MHS NYPL	
Dedication Service, 16p.	Exeter	1801	LM	
16p. 8vo.	Salem	1804	Harv	

Hark from the Tombs

12p. obl.	Exeter	1800	LM LOC

Harmonia Americana

120p. obl.	Boston	1791	AAS LM
			LOC W

Hymn for the New Year	n. p.	n. d.	LM

Instrumental Assistant, Vol. 1

	c1800	Mass. CR
Second ed.	c1816	Mass. CR

Same, Vol. 2	Exeter	1807	BPL

(Both volumes in one in LOC)

Massachusetts Compiler Boston	1795	

See Hans Gram

Miscellaneous Collection of Anthems 1793 LM
Miscellaneous Collection of Sacred Music n. d. LM
Occasional Companion in twelve numbers

No. 1 & 2	Salem		Harv.
No. 1, 3, 5, 7			LM
No. 7, paged 111-120			
	Boston	n. d.	AAS
Occasional Music, 11p.	Exeter	1802	Harv

Vocal Companion

174p. obl.	Exeter	1807	LM
			LOC NYPL

HOUGH, GEORGE
    Modern Harmony   1808

Howe, Solomon
    Divine Hymns   Greenwich   1805
    Farmers Evening Entertainment
        32p. obl.   Northampton   1804 LOC MHS
    Worshipper's Assistant
        32p. obl.   Northampton 1799 (c1800)
                  AAS BPL LM LOC NYPL
Hubbard, John (1750-1810)
    Harmonia Selecta   Worcester   1789
    Thirty Anthems selected by
                 Newburyport 1814 AAS LM
Huntington, Jonathan (1771-1838)
    Apollo Harmony
        128p. 8vo.   Northhampton 1807 LOC
    Classical Sacred Music
        75p. 8vo.   Boston   1812 AAS
                                  Harv W
Husband, Jenkins John (1753?-1809?)
    Collection of Hymns and Psalms
                 Lancaster, Pa. 1807
Ingalls, Jeremiah (1764-1828)
    Christian Harmony, or Songster's Companion
        144p.   Exeter   1805 AAS
                            BPL Harv
Jackson, Dr. George K. (1745-1823)
    A Choice Collection of Chants
                 n. p.   1816 AAS
    Choral Companion   Boston   1817 LM
Janes, Walter (1779-1827)
    Harmonic Minstrelsy Dedham   1807 BPL
                                    LM MHS

Massachusetts Harmony
      125p.   Boston   1803 BPL

JENKS, STEPHEN (1772-1856)
    American Compiler Northampton 1803
    Delights of Harmony
      68p. obl. New Haven 1804 LOC
    Delights of Harmony, or Norfolk Compiler
      110p   Dedham 1805 AAS
                LM MHS
    Delights of Harmony, or Union Compiler, No. 2
         Dedham 1806 LM
    Harmony of Zion, or Union Compiler
      80p. obl. Dedham 1818 AAS BPL
                LM MHS RIHS
    Hartford Collection of Sacred Harmony, with Elijah Gris-
      wold and John C. Frisbie
      60p.   Hartford 1807 BPL
    New England Harmonist
      16p.   New Haven 1800
     Second ed. 40p. (set in type) 1803
    Royal Harmony of Zion Dedham 1810
    Zion's Harp   New York 1824

JOCELYN, SIMEON (1746-1823)
    Chorister's Companion, with Amos Doolittle
      2, 20, 64p. obl. New Haven 1782 LOC MHS
     Second ed.
      26, 2, 120p. obl. New Haven 1788 EI LM
                MHS NYPL BPL
     Second ed. corrected and enlarged 1791 Evans
     Supplement, corrected and enlarged
      16p. obl. c1791 but printed in 1792 LOC MHA W

Second part
8, 72p. obl.   New Haven   1790   Evans
Second part corrected and enlarged
obl.   New Haven   1791   Evans
Part Third 16, 32p. obl. New Haven n. d.
bound at end of Part Second   1782 W
Favorite Psalm Tunes
16p.   obl.   New Haven   1787   Evans
Federal Harmony   Boston   1793

JOHNSTON, THOMAS
Tunes   1753   MHS
(Bound with a Tate and Brady of 1763)
Same, 17p.   Boston   1755   JCB
Same 16 leaves   NYPL
(With the New England Psalm Book of 1758)
Same   Boston   1760

KEATING, HENRY S.
Key to Harmony
86p. small 8vo. Baltimore   1808   MdHS

KENT, EMANUEL
David's Harp
Second ed. enlarged and improved, engraved music
9-128p.   Baltimore   n. d.   AAS   LM

KIMBALL, JACOB, SAMUEL HOLYOKE and others
Essex Harmony, Part 1   c1802 Mass. CR

KIMBALL, JACOB, JR. (1761-1826)
Essex Harmony, 112p.   Exeter   1800   AAS   BPL
Congl LM   MHS

Rural Harmony
112p.   obl.   Exeter   1793   AAS   LM
LOC   MHS   NYPL

THE

FEDERAL HARMONY:

IN THREE PARTS.

CONTAINING,

I. AN INTRODUCTION to the Grounds of MUSICK.
II. A large Collection of celebrated PSALM and HYMN TUNES from the most approved ancient and modern Authors : Together with several new ones, never before published : Suited to all Metres usually sung in Churches.
III. Select ANTHEMS, &c. &c.

Compiled for the Use of SCHOOLS and SINGING SOCIETIES.

O Praise ye the LORD, prepare your glad Voice : In our Great CREATOR, let Isr'el Rejoice Psalm cxlix.

BOSTON: Printed and Sold by JOHN NORMAN at his Office No. 75, Newbury-street.   MDCCXC.

Federal Harmony, 1790, by Timothy Swan

From copy in the Library of Congress

LANGDON, CHAUNCEY (1764-1830)
　　Beauties of Psalmody
　　　　　56p.　obl.　　　(New Haven)　1786　AAS
LANE, ISAAC
　　Anthem for Ordination　Northampton　1797　Rarv
LAW, ANDREW (1748-1821)
　　Art of Playing the Organ
　　　　　8p.　　　　　Philadelphia　1809　EI
　　Same　　　　　　　　　　　　　1819
　　Art of Singing, in three parts, each part separately paged,
　　　　　obl.　　　　　Cheshire　　1794　LOC
　　　Second ed. 224p. (The only edition paged consecutively)
　　　　　obl.　　　　　Cheshire　　1800　LOC
　　　Fourth ed. (so-called, really the Third ed., part 1 only)
　　　　　96p.　obl.　　Cambridge　　1803　LOC
　　　　　(Printed in his "new notation" of four characters)
　　　　　(Other copies are in MHS　NYPL　Harv)
　　Fourth ed.　　　　　Windsor, Vt.　1805
　　　　　　　　　　　Philadelphia　1810
　　Vol. II　　　　　　Salem　　　　1796　LM
　　Part II.—See Christian Harmony
　　Part III.—See The Musical Magazine
　　Christian Harmony; Part II. of the Art of Singing in two
　　　　volumes
　　　Vol. I, 64p.　obl.　bound as Part II of The Art of Singing
　　　　　　　　　　　Cheshire　　1794　LOC　Harv
　　　Vol. II 56p.　obl.　Cheshire　　1794　Priv
　　　Vol. II 56p.　obl.　Cheshire　　1796　LOC
　　　　　(Also as p. 97-160 obl. Windsor, Vt. in the 1803 edi-
　　　　　tion of The Art of Singing, LOC)
　　　Third ed.
　　　Fourth ed.　　　　Windsor　　　1805

33

Collection of Hymns for Social Worship

        36p.   Cheshire   1782

        48p.   Cheshire   1783(?) LOC

      bound with his Tunes

Collection of Best Tunes and Anthems

        no title   New Haven   1779 NYPL

                        New Haven   1781 Evans

                        Cheshire   1782 Evans

Collection of Hymn Tunes

        36p.   Cheshire   1782 LOC

                        Cheshire   1786 Evans

                        Cheshire   1792 Evans

Essay on Music, 24p.   Philadelphia   1814 LOC

Harmonic Companion

        120p. obl.   Philadelphia   1807 EI

                                                    MHS Yale

Harmonic Companion, 112p. obl.

    followed by The Art of Playing the Organ, 8p., c1809

    then 113-120p. of music, Philadelphia, n. d., c1807 Priv

Second ed. obl.   Philadelphia

Third ed. obl.   Philadelphia   1810

Fourth ed. 120p. obl. Philadelphia   1819 LOC

Musical Magazine No. 1

        64p. obl.   Cheshire   1792 LM LOC

No. 2   Cheshire   1793 LOC MHS

    (There were two issues of this number)

No. 3   Baltimore   1793

No. 4   Baltimore   1795

    (Four numbers bound together in LM)

No. 5   1799 CR

No. 6   Nov. 1801 LM

    (Also as p. 209-224 in The Art of Singing 1800 LOC)

Fourth ed. of the six numbers on

96p. obl.   Boston   1805 LOC

Musical Primer   New Haven   1780 Evans

                                .. (doubtful)

First ed. 32p. obl.   Cheshire   1793 LOC
  ("Copy of First Edition in original paper covers")

Second ed. 32p. obl. Cheshire   1794 LOC
  (bound with his Art of Singing 1794 and separately paged)

Third ed. bound in the 1800 edition of The Art of Singing
                                     LOC

Third ed. (separate) Philadelphia   1812 NYPL

Fourth ed. 64p. in Law's "notation" in the 1803 edition
  of The Art of Singing LOC

Rudiments of Music

48p. obl.   Cheshire   1783 LOC

Second ed.   Cheshire   1785

Third ed.   Cheshire   1791 Evans

Fourth ed. 6, 76p.   Cheshire   1792 LOC

                                   NŶPL MHS

  (Timothy Swan's copy of this edition is in the library
    of the Harvard Musical Association)

Fourth ed. 76p. obl. Cheshire   1793 W

Supplement to The Musical Primer, in his "new notation"
  of seven characters   1811 CR

     64p. obl.   Philadelphia 1811 W

Select Harmony   Cheshire   1778

     98p.   Farrington, Ct. 1779 LOC

     8, 100p. obl. New Haven   1779 Evans

  ("W" copy, which appears to be of this edition, has
    n. p., n. d.)

                 Baltimore   1784

(A pirated edition printed by Danied Bayley at Newburyport, 1784)

    8, 100p. obl. Baltimore   1786 Evans
                  Cheshire   1791 Evans
                  Cheshire   1792 Evans

An imperfect copy with no title in EI

A copy with 100p. but no date in LOC

Select Number of Plain Tunes

    16p.   Boston   1767 Evans
                  Boston   1772 Evans
    16p.   Boston   1773 W

    with a Tate and Brady

    16p.   Boston   1775 LOC

Same bound with a Tate and Brady of 1774 BPL

Same bound with a Watt's Psalms of 1781 NYPL

(Some one has facetiously said that Law must have
carried a printing press around with him, and
printed selections of his compositions to suit his
wants at the time. Certain it is that he issued
numerous editions of most of his compilations)

LEE, THOMAS, JR.

    Sacred Harmony

        12 99p. obl. Boston   1790 Evans

LESLIE, BENJAMIN

    Concert Harmony, or Youth's Assistant

        136p.   Salem   1811 NYPL

LEWIS, FREEMAN (1780-1859)

    Beauties of Harmony   (c1813)

    Second ed. 194p. Pittsburg   1816 AAS

LITTLE, HENRY

    Wesleyan Harmony

        128p. obl. Hallowell, Me. 1820 W

Second ed. 144p. obl.　Hallowell, Me.　1821　W

Little, William and William Smith

The Easy Instructor　Philadelphia　1798　(doubtful)
　　　　104p.　obl.　Albany (c1802) n. d.　LOC
Rev. ed.　　　　　　Albany　　　n. d.　LOC
　　　　108p.　obl.　Albany　　　1806　Priv
　　　　　　　　　　Albany　　　1807
　　　　108p.　obl.　Albany　　　1808　AAS
　　　　112p.　obl.　Albany　　　(1810) LOC
Rev. & enl. 127p. obl.　Albany　　n. d.　LOC
　　　　　　　　　　　　　　　　1812
　　　　　　　　　　　　　　　　1814
　　　　　　　　　　Albany　　　1816
　　　　　　　　　　Harrisburg, Pa.　1818
　　　　　　　　　　Utica　　　　1818　LM
　　　　　　　　　　Albany　　　1818
　　　　　　　　　　Albany　　　1820
　　　　　　　　　　Utica　　　　1820　NYPL
Revised and enlarged edition
　　　　128p.　obl.　Albany　n. d. (1825?)　Priv
　　　　128p.　obl.　Albany　　　1828　Priv
　　　　135p.　obl.　Albany　　　1831　AAS
　　　(There were probably many other editions)

Loud, Thomas (?-1834)

The Psalmist 64p. 8vo.　Philadelphia　1824　Harv

Lyon, James (1735-1794)

Urania　198p. obl.　Philadelphia　1761　LOC NYPL
　　　obl.　　　　　Philadelphia　1761　BPL
　　differs from the above
Second ed. 198p. obl.　Philadelphia　1767　YC
Third ed. 198p. obl.　Philadelphia　1773　NYHS
Fourth ed. 198p. obl.　Philadelphia　n. d.　MHS

MADAM, REV. MARTIN (1726-1790)

Lock Hospital Collection, first published in London, 1769

Reprint from the last London edition

200p. large obl. Boston, Mass.　1809　AAS　Harv

MANN, ELIAS (1750-1825)

Massachusetts Collection

191p.	obl.	Boston	1807	AAS	LM
200p.	obl.	Boston	1807	LOC	

Northampton Collection

		Northampton	1778		
139p.	obl.	Northampton	1797	Congl	LOC
140p.	obl.	Northampton	1802	LOC	

MASON, LOWELL (1792-1872)

Boston Handel and Haydn Society's Collection of Church
　Music　　　　　　　　　　　　c1820　Mass.　CR

323p.	obl.	Boston	1822	Priv	

Second ed.　　　　　　　　　c1823　Mass.　CR

Third ed.　　　　　　　　　c1825　Mass.　CR

Fourth ed.

Fifth ed.

Sixth ed.

Seventh ed. with additions and improvements

360p.　obl.　　Boston　　　1829　Priv

Eighth ed.

Ninth ed.

Tenth ed. 360p.　obl.　Boston　　　1830　Priv

Eleventh ed.

Twelfth ed. 360p. obl.　Boston　　　1832　W

Thirteenth ed.

360p.　obl.　　Boston　　　1833　W

Fourteenth ed.　　　　　　　1834　Priv.

Fifteenth ed.

Sixteenth ed.
Seventeenth ed.   1837   Priv
Eighteenth ed.   1838   Priv
Vol. 2   c1822   Mass.   CR
Vol. 2   c1823   Mass.   CR

MASSACHUSETTS COLLECTION
     105p.   Greenfield   1823   BPL   Congl

MASSACHUSETTS HARMONY, by a lover of harmony
     (Sometimes attributed to William Billings and to
       Andrew Law)
     95p. obl.   Boston   (1784) W   n.d.
  Second ed. 101p. obl.   Boston   1785   Evans

MAXIM, ABRAHAM (1773-1829)
  Northern Harmony   c1804   Maine   CR
       Hallowell   1808
  Second ed.   Hallowell   1816
  Third ed.
  Fourth ed. improved and enlarged   c1816   Maine   CR
  Fifth ed. 142p. obl.   Hallowell   1819   LOC
  Oriental Harmony
     56p. obl.   Exeter   1802   LOC

MAXIM, JOHN
     A manuscript collection of his music is in the MHS

McCULLOUGH, JOHN
  Selected Music   Philadelphia   1805

MERRILL, DAVID
  Psalmodist's Best Companion, 72 p.   n. d.   MHS

METCALF, SAMUEL L. (1798-1856)
  Kentucky Harmonist   c1817
    Second ed. 130p. obl.   Cincinnati   1820   Priv
    Third ed.
    Fourth ed. 128p. obl.   Cincinnati   (c1817) 1826   WR

MIDDLESEX COLLECTION OF SACRED MUSIC

136p. obl.	Boston	1807	LOC
			MHS RIHS
Second ed. 168p. obl.	Boston	1808	LOC
Third ed. 160p. obl.	Boston	1811	BPL
			Congl LOC

MILLARD, CLEMENT

United States Harmony   c1810   Penn   CR

MILLENNIAL PRAISES. A Collection of Gospel Hymns copyrighted
      by Josiah Tallcott, Junr.   c1814   Mass.   CR

MILLER, H.

Hymn Book for children of the Brethren's Congregation
      (Perhaps no music)   Philadelphia   1763

MITCHELL, NAHUN (1769-1853)

LXXX Psalm and Hymn Tunes
               Boston   1810   LM   LOC
      (Also known as the Brattle Street Collection)

A Hymn Tune   1813   MHS

Lord's Day, a hymn tune
    Second ed.
    Third ed.
    Fourth ed.   6p.   Boston   1817   LOC   MHS
    Fifth ed.   Boston   1823

MODERN COLLECTION OF SACRED MUSIC
         254p.   Boston   1800   BPL

MOORS, HEZEKIAH

Province Harmony
         140p. obl.   Boston   1809   MHS

NEVIUS, J. W., with Cornelius Vandeventer and John Frazee

New Brunswick Collection
         72p. obl.   New Bruns-
                    wick, N. J.   1817   AAS   LOC

AN ORIGINAL COLLECTION

OF

PSALM TUNES,

EXTRACTED FROM THE BEAUTIFUL WORKS, (CHIEFLY SACRED) OF THE MOST CELEBRATED

ANCIENT AND MODERN COMPOSERS,

TO WHICH ARE ADDED SEVERAL TUNES COMPOSED EXPRESSLY FOR THIS WORK.

The whole arranged for Three Voices, and adapted to the Metres of Dr. Watt's Psalms and Hymns.

BY ARTHUR CLIFTON,

ORGANIST OF THE FIRST PRESBYTERIAN CHURCH OF BALTIMORE.

Baltimore: Printed for the Author, and to be had of him, No. 4, S. Gay-street, and at T. Carr's Music Store.

PRINTED BY T. MURPHY, 2, SOUTH GAY-STREET.

Psalm Tunes, 1820, by Arthur Clifton

From a copy owned by a correspondent in Baltimore

Second ed.

Third ed. 120p. obl. New Bruns-
              wick, N. J. 1822 W

Fourth ed. 128p. obl. New Bruns-
              wick, N. J. 1827 AAS

(This and succeeding editions were compiled by Cornelius Vandeventer)

Fifth ed. 136p.   New Bruns-
              wick, N. J. 1829 AAS

Sixth ed. 144p.   New Bruns-
              wick, N. J. 1832 AAS

Seventh ed. 160p.   New Bruns-
              wick, N. J. 1835 AAS

Eighth ed. 188p.   New Bruns-
               wick, N. J. 1840 AAS

NEWHALL, JAMES

    Vocal Harmony, 24p.   Northampton   1803 BPL

NEW HAVEN COLLECTION

         144p. obl.   Dedham   1818 BPL LOC

OLD COLONY COLLECTION OF ANTHEMS, two volumes

                  Boston   1818 Harv

    Same Vol. I.   Boston   1818 LOC

    Same Vol. II.   c1819 Mass. CR

    Third ed.   c1823 Mass. CR

OLMSTED, TIMOTHY

    Musical Olio, 112p. obl. Northampton 1805 AAS BPL
                                        LOC NYPL

    Second ed. improved and enlarged, published at Hartford
    but printed at New London
        127p. obl.   1811 AAS
                                          LOC NYPL

PALFREY, WARWICK (1787-1838)
    Evangelical Psalmodist
            56p. obl.   Salem   1802 BPL
                                                     LM LOC
PATTERSON, ROBERT
    Church Music
        Second ed.   Pittsburg   1815 LM
PEARSON, JOHN
    Dedication Service, 6p. Salem   1805 Harv.
PECK, DANIEL L.
    Musical Medley, 104p.   Dedham   1808 AAS
    Selection of Sacred Music
            104p.   Philadelphia   1810 AAS W
PETERS, ABSALOM (1793-1869)
    Sacred Music   1823
PILLSBURY, AMOS
    United States Sacred Harmony
            224p. obl.   Boston   1799 LOC
                             Charleston, S. C.   AAS
PLAIN PSALMODY—See Oliver Holden, Boston, 1800   LOC
POOL, DAVID—See Josiah Holbrook
POOR, JOHN
    Psalms and Hymns for a Young Ladies' Academy
            48p.   Philadelphia   1794 AAS
                                                     LM W
PORTSMOUTH COLLECTION OF SACRED MUSIC
            134p. obl.   Exeter   1814 LM LOC
PSALMS AND HYMNS WITH TUNES
        (Pages cut)   Exeter   1817
            Date 1817 quoted from Warrington, but probably the
            same as "Valuable Collection" 1818, which see

42

PSALM TUNES FOR CHRIST CHURCH AND SAINT PETERS CHURCH
Philadelphia   1763

PSALMS OF DAVID FOR THE DUTCH REFORMED CHURCH

    Printed by John Parker, New York   1767 LOC JCB
    (First music printed in America from type)

READ, DANIEL (1757-1836)

    American Musical Miscellany

Northampton   1798

    American Singing Book

73p. obl.	New Haven	1785	LOC
Second ed.	New Haven	(1788)	Evans
Third ed.	New Haven	1792	Evans
Fourth ed. 16p. obl.	New Haven	1793	LOC MHS
Supplement	New Haven	(1787)	W

    American Musical Magazine

Vol. I.	New Haven	(1786-7)	Yale

    Columbian Harmonist No. I.

40p. obl.	New Haven	1793	AAS LOC MHS Yale
Second ed. 95p. obl.	Dedham	1804	NECons
Third ed.	Dedham	1806	LM RIHS HU
Third ed.	Boston	1807	NYPL
Fourth ed. 112p. obl.	Boston	1810	AAS LOC
No. 2, 40p.	New Haven		BPL Yale
No. 3, 39p. obl.	New Haven	1795	LM LOC
No. 4		1810	LM
Supplement 32p. bound alone n. p.		n. d.	LOC

    Introduction to Psalmody

	New Haven	1790	Evans

    New Haven Collection

144p. obl.	Dedham	1818	LOC

43

READ, JOEL (1753-(   )

New England Selection or Plain Psalmodist

                      Boston   1808 MHS

Second ed. 128p. obl. Boston   1812 AAS LM

                                            LOC NECons

Supplement of 24p. added to Daniel Read's Columbian
Psalmodist, Second ed. 1804 in NECons

REED, EPHRAIM

Musical Monitor, or New York Collection

        199p. 8vo.   Ithaca   1820 LOC

Second ed.   c1822 N.Y. CR

Third ed. revised and improved

        232p. 8vo.   Ithaca   1824 LOC

Fourth rev. ed. enlarged and improved

        248p.   Ithaca   1825 AAS

Fifth ed. revised and improved

        248p. obl.   Ithaca   1827 LOC

RILEY, E.

Sacred Melodies, original and selected c1817 N.Y. CR

ROBBINS, CHARLES

Columbian Harmony, or Maine Collection of Church Music

        208p. obl.   Exeter   1805 LOC RIHS

ROBERTS, ELI

Hartford Collection

        187p. obl.   New London 1812 AAS LM

RUSS, D.

Uranian Harmony, 76p. Philadelphia   1791 Evans

SALEM COLLECTION OF CLASSICAL SACRED MUSIC

        124p. obl.   Salem   1805 BPL   Harv

SANGER, ZEDEKIAH (1771-1821)

Meridian Harmony

        110p. obl.   Dedham   1808 BPL

                                          LM LOC

SCHAFFER, FRANCIS C.

Hymns set to Music

          68p. square   Boston   1811 AAS

SELECT HARMONY, being the Fourth Part of Samuel Worcester's
    Christian Psalmody,

          48p. 8vo.   Boston   1813 BPL

    Second ed. 80p. 8vo.   1817 Priv

SELECTION OF PSALM TUNES for the use of the Protestant Episco-
    pal Church in the State of New York

                              c1812 N.Y. CR

SELECTION OF SACRED HARMONY, printed for William Young
    Second ed.
    Third ed.
    Fourth ed. greatly impr. and enl.

          132p. obl.   Philadelphia   1794 AAS

SEYMOUR, LEWIS and
SEYMOUR, THADDEUS

    The Musical Instructor   c1803 N.Y. CR

    New York Selection of Sacred Music

          62p.   New York   1809 NYPL

    Same   New York   1812

    Same   New York   1816 LM

SHAW, OLIVER (1779-1848)

    Melodia Sacra, or Providence Selection

          152p. obl.   Providence   1819 AAS BPL
                                      LM LOC RIHS

      Another edition with appendix

          168p. obl.   Providence   1819 Priv W

    Providence Selection   Providence   1815

        (Doubtful if printed at Providence)

    Same, 128p. 8vo.   Dedham   1815 AAS BPL
                                    LM LOC RIHS W

SHAW, OLIVER, with Amos Albee and Herman Mann
Columbian Sacred Harmonist
126p. obl. Dedham 1808 LM LOC
MHS W
SHUMWAY, NEHEMIAH
American Harmony
212p. obl. Philadelphia 1793 LOC W
220p. obl. Philadelphia 1801 LOC
SMITH, REV. WILLIAM
Chants for Public Worship 1814
Churchman's Choral Companion
8, 45p. New York 1809 Harv LM
Easy Instructor, Part II.
Second ed. preface dated Hopewell, N. J. 1806
72p. obl. AAS
(See also William Little)
SMITH AND PRELLEUR
The Harmonious Companion 1732
SOUTHGATE, CHARLES
Harmonia Sacra c1818 CR
STICKNEY, JOHN (1744-1827)
Gentleman's and Ladies' Musical Companion
12, 220p. obl. Newburyport 1774 BPL LOC
212p. obl. Newburyport (1776) LOC
Newburyport 1783 Evans
(MHS and NYPL have undated copies)
STONE, JOSEPH, with Abraham Wood
Columbian Harmony
112p. obl. n. p. 1793 LOC
SUFFOLK SELECTION OF CHURCH MUSIC
160p. Boston 1807 AAS Congl
LOC

46

SWAN, TIMOTHY (1758-1842)
Federal Harmony obl. Boston   1785   Evans
           obl.   Boston   1788   MHS
      114p. obl.   Boston   1790   AAS   LOC
      130p. obl.   Boston   1792   Evans
                                        Catalogue

New England Harmony
      103p. obl.   Northampton   1801   Harv
                                    MHS   LOC

Songster's Assistant
      36p.   Suffield   1800   BPL
Songster's Museum   Northampton   1803   BPL
SEENEY, GEORGE C., with William Cooper
   Sacred Music, 71p.   Boston   1810   LOC   W
TANS'UR, WILLIAM—See Daniel Bayley
TEMPLI CARMINA—See Bridgewater Collection
TERRIL, ISRAEL
   Vocal Harmony, No. I.
      64p. obl.   New Haven   (1805) LM   LOC
      (The owner of the copy in LOC has written the date
         1805)
THOMSON, SAMUEL
   Columbian Harmony
      44p.   Dedham   1810   MHS
TOMLINS, J.
   Sacred Music, No. I.   Boston   1810
TRINITY CHURCH HYMNS. Pages 161-174 tunes
      small 8vo.   Boston   1808   W
TUFTS, REV. JOHN (1689-1750)
   Introduction to the Art of Singing
                 Boston   1715   Evans
   Second ed.

Third ed.
Fourth ed.
Fifth ed. 12p.
    small 8vo.   Boston   1726 BPL
Sixth ed.
Seventh ed. 12p.
    small 8vo.   Boston   1728 AAS
Eighth ed. small 8vo. Boston   1731 MHS
Ninth ed. 8p.
    imp. small 8vo. Boston   1736 EI
Tenth ed. 12p.
    small 8vo.   Boston   1738 NYPL
Eleventh ed.   Boston   1744

TUNES SUITED TO THE PSALMS AND HYMNS OF THE BOOK OF COM-
    MON PRAYER   Philadelphia 1786
TURNER, JAMES
    Tunes, bound with Barnard's Psalms
        16p.   Boston   1752 Harv MHS
URANIAN SOCIETY, LESSONS FOR THE
              Philadelphia 1785
    Same   Philadelphia 1787
URANIAN HARMONY
        134p. obl.   Boston   n. d. LOC
VALUABLE COLLECTION OF SACRED MUSIC
        254p.   Exeter   1818 Priv
    (This is the lower part of a book whose leaves are cut
        across, the upper part being The Psalms of David)
VAN DEVENTER, CORNELIUS—See John W. Nevius
VILLAGE HARMONY, or The Youth's Assistant 1798
    Second ed.
    Third ed.
    Fourth ed. 202p. obl. Exeter   1798 W

THE
ROYAL MELODY COMPLETE:
OR THE
NEW HARMONY of ZION.

CONTAINING

I. A *New* and *Correct* INTRODUCTION to the *Grounds* of MUSICK, *Rudimental, Practical* and *Technical*.
II. A *New* and *Complete* Body of CHURCH-MUSICK, adapted to the most select *Portions* of the Book of PSALMS, of either *Versions*; with many *Fuging Chorus's*, and *Gloria Patri's* to the Whole.
III. A New and Select *Number* of HYMNS, ANTHEMS, and CANONS, suited to several Occasions; and many of them never before printed; Set by the greatest *Masters* in the World.

The Whole are Composed in *Two, Three, Four*, and *Five Musical Parts*, according to the nicest *Rules*; consisting of *Solo's, Fuges*, and *Chorus's*, correctly set in Score for *Voices* or *Organ*; and fitted for all *Teachers, Learners*, and Musical SOCIETIES, *&c.* with a Preface on *Church-Musick*, shewing the Beauty and Excellency thereof.

The THIRD EDITION, with Additions.

By WILLIAM TANS'UR, Senior, *Musico Theorico*.

Psf. cxlix. { *O Praise ye the* LORD, *prepare your glad* Voice; *His Praise in the Great Assembly to sing;* } Ver. 1.
{ *In our Great* CREATOR. *let lisp'el rejoice; And Children of* ZION *be glad in their* KING. }

BOSTON: Printed and sold by W. M'ALPINE, almost Mid-way betwixt the *Governor's* and Dr. *Gardener's,* *Marlborough-street*; also, sold by D. BAYLEY at *Newbury-Port*; and M. WILLIAMS at *Salem*. MDCCLXVII.

Royal Melody Complete, third edition, 1767, by William Tans'ur

From copy in the Library of Congress

Fifth ed.	206p. obl. Exeter	1800	LOC	
Sixth ed.	206p. obl. Exeter	1803	LOC	MHS
Seventh ed.	223p. obl. Exeter	1806	LOC	
Eighth ed.	230p. obl. Exeter	1807	BPL	LOC

Ninth ed.

Tenth ed.	Exeter	n. d.	AAS	

Eleventh ed.

326p. obl.	Newburyport	1812	BPL	LOC
Eleventh ed.	Exeter	1813	AAS	BPL
			EI	NYPL
Twelfth ed.	Newburyport	1815	BPL	MHS
Twelfth ed.	Exeter	1815	AAS	BPL
			MHS	NYPL

Thirteenth ed.

350p. obl.	Newburyport	1816	LOC

Fourteenth ed.

350p. obl.	Boston	1817	BPL	LOC

(Has sub-title, New England Repository of Sacred
Music)

Fifteenth ed.	Exeter	1818	AAS	

Sixteenth ed. revised and improved

347, (3)p. obl. Exeter	1819	AAS	Harv
		LOC	MHS

VILLAGE HARMONY, or New England Repository of Sacred Music
Seventeenth ed.

350p. obl.	Exeter	1820	LOC
Same		1821	BPL

WAINWRIGHT, REV. JONATHAN M. (1792-1854)
Set of Chants for the Protestant Episcopal Church

50p. 8vo.	Boston	1819	LOC

THE

Grounds and Rules

O F

MUSICK

Explained: Or,

An *Introduction* to the Art of Singing

by *N O T E.*

Fitted to the meaneſt Capacities.

By THOMAS WALTER. M.A.

Recommended by ſeveral Miniſters.

Let every thing that hath Breath praiſe the Lord. Pſal. 150. 6.

BOSTON : Printed by *J. Franklin*, for *S. Gerriſh*, near the Brick Church in Cornhill. 1721.

Grounds and Rules of Music, first edition, 1721, by Thomas Walter
From copy in the New York Public Library

WALTER, THOMAS (1696-1725)
Grounds and Rules of Music

16p.	obl.	Boston	1721	NYPL MHS LOC photostat
Second ed.	obl.	Boston	1723	photostat title in LOC
Imperfect (no title)			1737	Yale
	obl.		1740	Evans
16p.	obl.	Boston	1746	AAS BPL MHS NYPL
24p.	obl.	Boston	1757-1760	AAS LOC
24p.	obl.	Boston	1760	LOC MHS W (18p.)
24p.	obl.	Boston	1764	LOC Yale

WARD, WILLIAM
The Gamut, or Scale of Music

Utica	1806	

WARRINER, SOLOMON (1778-1860)
Springfield Collection

150p.   obl. Published at Springfield,
          printed at Boston   1813   AAS   Congl

WASHBURN, JAPHET COOMBS
Parish Harmony, or Fairfax Collection c1813   CR
Temple Harmony   c1818   CR
  Second ed.
  Third ed.   c1821   CR

WESLEYAN SELECTION OF JOHN STREET CHURCH
          92p.   obl.   New York   1820   LOC
WEST, ELISHA
The Musical Concert
          103p.   Northampton   1802   AAS

WEST CHURCH, A Collection of Sacred Music for

48p. obl.	Boston	1810	W	
80p. obl.	Boston	1810	AAS	BPL

WILLARD, SAMUEL (1776-1859)

Deerfield Collection	Northampton	c1814	CR	
135p. obl.	Northampton	n. d.	AAS	Congl
144p. obl.	Greenfield	1814	AAS	LOC
Second ed. 180p.	Greenfield	1818	AAS	
Regular Hymns with musical directions	c1823	CR		

WILLIAMS, AARON—See Daniel Bayley

WINCHELL, JAMES M. (1791-1820)

Sacred Harmony, 120p.	Boston	1819	LM	LOC

WOOD, ABRAHAM (1752-1804)

Columbian Harmony, with Joseph Stone

112p. obl.	n. p.	1793	LOC	
Divine Songs	Boston	1789	AAS	Yale
Funeral Elegy	Boston	1800	AAS	

Hymn of Peace, 8 leaves

engraved	Worcester	1784	BPL

WOOD, WILLIAM

Harmonia Evangelica

110p. obl.	Exeter	1810	LOC

WOODRUFF, MERIT N.

Devotional Harmony, 9-60 p. engraved	1800	Priv

WOODWARD AND AIKEN

Ecclesia Harmonia	c1806	CR
(see below)		

WOODWARD, CHARLES

Ecclesia Harmonia	Philadelphia	c1807	CR	
Second ed. 108p. obl.	Philadelphia	1809	AAS	LOC
			MHS	W

Sacred Music in Miniature
        208p. small obl. Philadelphia   1812 Harv

WORCESTER COLLECTION
        104p. obl.   Worcester   1786 AAS W
    Second ed. 120p. obl. Worcester   1788 AAS MHS
    Third ed. obl.   Boston   1791 AAS W
    Fourth ed. 152p. obl. Boston   1792 AAS MHS
    Fifth ed. 156p. obl. Boston   1794 AAS
                                           MHS Congl
    Sixth ed. 143p. obl. Boston   1797 AAS
                                         MHS Yale
      (This and succeeding editions were edited by Oliver
        Holden)
    Seventh ed. 144p. obl. Boston   1800 AAS MHS
    Eighth ed. 120p. and appendix 79p.
        obl.   Boston   1803 AAS LM
                              LOC MHS RIHS

WORCESTER COLLECTION, Part III
        200p. obl.   1787 AAS
                  Worcester   1788 AAS

WORCESTER, SAMUEL
    Select Harmony, bound with his Christian Psalmody
        (See Select Harmony)

WRIGHT, D.
    American Musical Miscellany   1798

WYETH, JOHN (1770-1858)
    Repository of Sacred Music
                  Harrisburg   1810
    Second ed.   Harrisburg   1812
    Third ed.
    Fourth ed. improved and corrected
                  Harrisburg   1818

Fifth ed. 130p. obl.	Harrisburg	1818	W
Fifth ed.	Harrisburg	1820	
Stereotyped ed., enlarged and improved			
144p. obl.	Harrisburg	1826	Harv W
Same	Harrisburg	1834	LOC W
Second Part			
132p. obl.	Harrisburg	1813	Priv W WR
Second ed. 132p. obl.	Harrisburg	1820	Priv LOC W

YOUNG, WILLIAM

Selection of Sacred Harmony		1790	Evans
	Philadelphia	1794	AAS

YOUNG MEN'S INSTRUCTIVE COMPANION

8,16p. obl. n. p.		n. d.	wrappers W